God is always there

////////////////////////

PSALMS FOR
EVERY MOMENT

////////////////////////

Kathleen Atkinson, OSB

Liguori
LIGUORI, MISSOURI

Imprimi Potest:
Harry Grile, CSsR, Provincial
Denver Province, The Redemptorists

Published by Liguori Publications
Liguori, Missouri 63057

To order, call 800-325-9521
www.liguori.org

Library of Congress Cataloging-in-Publication Data

Atkinson, Kathleen.
  God is always there / Kathleen Atkinson. — 1st ed.
    p. cm.
  ISBN 978-0-7648-2158-5
  1. Bible. O.T. Psalms—Meditations. I. Title.
  BS1430.54.A85 2012
  223'.206—dc23

                                         2012010085

Liguori Publications, a nonprofit corporation, is an apostolate of the Redemptorists. To learn more about the Redemptorists, visit Redemptorists.com.

Printed in the United States of America
16 15 14 13 12 / 5 4 3 2 1
First Edition

dedication

I gratefully dedicate this book to
Susan Berger, OSB, and Joanne Graham, OSB—
leaders, mentors, God-seekers,
faithful women of Annunciation Monastery,
Bismarck, North Dakota.

introduction

YOU MAY WANT to open this book and simply begin reading. Or you may want to look through the chapter titles and pay attention to the desire of your heart—What do you feel most? Do you want to laugh? Cry out? Lead?

However you choose to experience this book is the right way for you. Your choice is a response to the invitation of God—God, who is already present; God, who has first loved us and invited our free response; God, who has been with us throughout all ages. With such a God, we can break into song or burst into tears or cry out in despair or give praise with full throat as did the people of the community out of which the psalms were composed.

Living authentically and faithfully is never easy. Natural disasters, the death of loved ones, and broken relationships can fill us with sorrow. The laughter of a child, the magnificence of a choir, and the thunder of the sky can fill us with joy. Life is not made up of distinct times of sorrow and times of joy. Rather, life simultaneously holds both sorrow and joy in a creative tension that can only find description in symbolic expression: in art, music, poetry, and dance.

For more than 4,000 years, the Book of Psalms has been the song offered by the believing community who lived out this vibrant reality that God dwells in all experiences, happy and sad. The people of ancient Israel lived their lives in praise and lament as the psalms provided a rhythm for all they encountered. Since then, communities throughout the world have continued this practice. Jewish and Christian men and women have shared the common prayer of the psalms for centuries. Monastics worldwide gather seven times a day to pray and reflect on the psalms.

I invite you to become part of this experience of the psalms "in stereo" as you let your heart beat as one with those who expressed their faith in these prayers long ago.

CHOOSE A REFLECTION The psalms in this book are divided into three sections: faith, hope, and love. Within each section, selections from several different psalms are offered. Allow yourself to be drawn into God's presence as you read and pray.

GENTLY PRAY A PSALM AND ALLOW YOURSELF TO LINGER Where did you feel called forth in longing, seeking, stretching for fulfillment? What words or phrases stood out beyond all others? What persons or memories were evoked? Pay attention to what you hear God saying.

READ THE STORY AND REFLECTION Laugh, smile, allow a tender tear. Muse, reflect, and come to a new insight about how all our hearts beat to the one Spirit of God.

PRAY THE PRAYER RESPONSE Allow your reflection to stir up personal words of prayer within you.

RESPOND, ACTING ON THE INVITATION FOR TODAY If you are inspired to act, rejoice and follow the Spirit's prompting.

Remember, God is there ahead of us.

contents

LIVING IN HOPE 50

//////////////
LIVING IN LOVE 91
//////////////

//////////////
CONCLUSION 128
//////////////

LIVING IN FAITH

Take delight in the Lord
and he will give you the desires of your heart.

PSALM 37:4

TO LIVE IN FAITH is our birthright rather than something we earn. It is a sacred gift for us to receive with open hands. It is a gift from God—from *God*—so how could we not welcome it fully? Yet sometimes we forget.

When we live in faith, we are able to stand tall when everyone around us is cowering. It is to live with deep faith as all around us changes. It is to live with a resounding *yes* when everyone around us says "no." Living in faith is the daily walk of those who live from the interior of their heart rather than from external circumstances.

As we lift up our souls with the psalmist, groan with thirst and ponder in amazement, we create space for prayer and a place for God within us. This is how it is possible to live in faith.

Living in faith means to believe in the transforming power of God and to move beyond fear into a new and uncharted way of living. Faith does not undo fear but unravels it little by little as a safe place is created where we can name it. That place is with God.

to yield fruit

Happy are those
who do not follow the advice of the wicked,
or take the path that sinners tread,
or sit in the seat of scoffers;
but their delight is in the law of the LORD,
and on his law they meditate day and night.
They are like trees
planted by streams of water,
which yield their fruit in its season,
and their leaves do not wither.
In all that they do, they prosper.

The wicked are not so,
but are like chaff that the wind drives away.
Therefore the wicked will not stand in the judgment,
nor sinners in the congregation of the righteous;
for the LORD *watches over the way of the righteous,*
but the way of the wicked will perish.

The family reunion was held at the same location each year. Dozens of family members came, and thousands of dollars were spent to provide a wonderful time for everyone.

One year when everyone came to share their final breakfast and farewells, one young man noticed his father quietly looking over the bill, then approaching the cashier for a short conversation. The restaurant had inadvertently charged too little.

The dad noticed it, pointed out the mistake, and paid the higher amount. It cost him an extra $50.00, but it gained him the respect of his son and taught more than any lecture on business ethics.

Like a tree planted near a stream of water, the children of this simple man watched him closely and drank of his goodness. He walked in the way of the Lord as best he could each day and with everyone he met.

He sought more to be faithful than to be noticed for his actions. His children noticed.

Divine Lawgiver, free me from the temptation to play games with the truth. Teach me to walk honestly and humbly in your way.

Today, notice acts of simple honesty.

///////////////

to rest

Offer right sacrifices,
and put your trust in the LORD.

There are many who say,
"O that we might see some good!
Let the light of your face shine on us, O LORD*!"*
You have put gladness in my heart
more than when their grain and wine abound.

I will both lie down and sleep in peace;
for you alone, O LORD*, make me lie down in safety.*

PSALM 4:5–8

It was a fantastic summer afternoon in the park, and everyone was enjoying a family soccer match with cousins, brothers, sisters, aunts, and uncles of all ages. After extensive running and laughter, one of the aunts held up her hand and called for a "time-out." Young Matt looked confused, then ran to his mother with huge tears in his eyes and said, "Mom, Aunt Karen gave me a time-out, but I don't know what I did."

A simple request for breath by a middle-aged aunt had been perceived as a punishment by the young boy.

We all need time-outs. Time to take a breath, time to reflect and be silent. Time to allow the light of God to shine upon us. Time to remember that it is the Lord alone who brings security to our lives.

Run—laugh—play—work diligently and plan responsibly.

Then take time out to remember that God alone is in charge.

Gentle God, receive my tired spirit. Anoint my weary body. Look upon my valiant efforts to care for others with tenderness and bring them to fruition. I entrust my work, my loved ones, my world, to you alone.

Today, sit quietly and feel your heart beat.
Be at one with yourself.

to stand amazed

O LORD, our Sovereign,
how majestic is your name in all the earth!

You have set your glory above the heavens.
Out of the mouths of babes and infants
you have founded a bulwark because of your foes,
to silence the enemy and the avenger.

When I look at your heavens, the work of your fingers,
the moon and the stars that you have established;
what are human beings that you are mindful of them,
mortals that you care for them?

Yet you have made them a little lower than God,
and crowned them with glory and honor.
You have given them dominion over the works of your hands;
you have put all things under their feet,
all sheep and oxen,
and also the beasts of the field,
the birds of the air, and the fish of the sea,
whatever passes along the paths of the seas.
O LORD, our Sovereign,
how majestic is your name in all the earth!

A young boy wrote the following letter:
"Dear God, we learned today in school that Thomas Edison invented light. But in Sunday school, we learned that you created it. I'll bet Edison got the idea from you, didn't he?"

All good ideas come from God.

It is easy to lose track of this truth. But what if we really looked?

What if we stood amazed at what we saw, heard, smelled, tasted, touched; marveled at the variety of animals, plants, landscapes; relished the adventure of living, loving, seeking, striving?

All good ideas come from God.

The greatest of these is us—a little less than God, yet crowned with glory and honor.

Now that's amazing!

Awesome God, I take my place in your amazing world. Hold me in your hand with the magnificence of all you have made. How majestic are you, O Lord our God.

Today, linger outside in the darkness of night.
Stand beneath the moon and the stars.
Imagine all the work of God's fingers.

PSALM 10
////////////////////

to win justice

Rise up, O Lord; O God, lift up your hand;
do not forget the oppressed.
Why do the wicked renounce God,
and say in their hearts, "You will not call us to account"?

But you do see! Indeed you note trouble and grief,
that you may take it into your hands;
the helpless commit themselves to you;
you have been the helper of the orphan.

Break the arm of the wicked and evildoers;
seek out their wickedness until you find none.
The Lord is king forever and ever;
the nations shall perish from his land.

O Lord, you will hear the desire of the meek;
you will strengthen their heart, you will incline your ear
to do justice for the orphan and the oppressed,
so that those from earth may strike terror no more.

PSALM 10:12–18

Edwin was eight years old and had the haunting look of a boy who had already seen too much pain. His home address showed on his face, where the dirt had probably been for days. The clothing he wore had not been washed since it had been claimed from the garbage truck.

Edwin and his family lived on the outskirts of the city dump. He had been conceived and born there, and would probably die there. He scavenged daily for food, clothing, and supplies to help build shelter for his family.

Fighting vultures for daily survival is an unthinkable way to live. Yet Edwin has known no other.

Edwin lives with the hope that a new day just might bring a new chance for a better life.

> Just and holy God, rise up and bring justice to your world. Defend the poor, plead the cause of the helpless, and break the bondage of the wicked. Challenge my indifference and use me as your weapon.

Today, remember the oppressed.
Do justice.

to dwell with God

O LORD, who may abide in your tent?
Who may dwell on your holy hill?

Those who walk blamelessly, and do what is right,
and speak the truth from their heart;
who do not slander with their tongue,
and do no evil to their friends,
nor take up a reproach against their neighbors;
in whose eyes the wicked are despised,
but who honor those who fear the LORD;
who stand by their oath even to their hurt;
who do not lend money at interest,
and do not take a bribe against the innocent.

Those who do these things shall never be moved.

The "Mothers' Club" began when they were all young moms. They shared their joys and challenges, studied the wisdom of the day, and encouraged one another in all that motherhood brought their way.

As their children grew and became teens, they continued to gather. Then they became grandmothers and shared the joy of watching their children raise their own children.

Over the years, the group changed. Some women moved to different cities and other women joined. The conversations changed from family matters to contemporary events and world travel.

Their children and grandchildren were still central, but now they discussed multiple doctor visits, bedside vigils at the hospital, and sought prayers for one another as they adjusted to living as widows.

Their decades of friendship continued with spirited Bridge games, twenty women became a dozen, and the hostess and driving duties were shared by those still physically able to do so. Eventually, several tables of card players became a foursome.

After more than 70 years, the Mothers' Club ended with the death of Edna, the last founding member. They had walked together through years of change and stayed faithful friends. Now they dwell with God and those they loved here on Earth.

God of all ages, I give you thanks for all those who have formed me and the life I now live. May they dwell in your tent, O Lord.

Today, write the names of those who have formed you most in life.

PSALM 19

to rejoice

The heavens are telling the glory of God;
and the firmament proclaims his handiwork.
Day to day pours forth speech,
and night to night declares knowledge.
There is no speech, nor are there words;
their voice is not heard;
yet their voice goes out through all the earth,
and their words to the end of the world.

In the heavens he has set a tent for the sun,
which comes out like a bridegroom from his wedding canopy,
and like a strong man runs its course with joy.
Its rising is from the end of the heavens,
and its circuit to the end of them;
and nothing is hidden from its heat.

PSALM 19:1–6

J oey is a really good kid. He's definitely all boy, but he's a really good kid." This was the mantra of Joey's dad. This was the opening line any time he was asked how the kindergarten parent program or a church event had gone, and his weary response when everyone piled out of the car for a family celebration after a five-hour drive.

Joey poured himself into life. He lived with excitement and an energy that lit up a room when he ran into it, seldom stopping to walk. Maybe that is why Jesus said to the apostle, "Let the children come to me."

"Let the children come to me," as they declare the glory of God's boundless creative energy.

"Let the children come to me," as they penetrate the humdrum routines into which life can settle.

"Let the children come to me," for theirs is the kingdom of God.

> Radiant God, you have pitched your tent among us, and our lives are forever changed. Continue to call us from mediocrity to passion and adventure. Your message is a message of life. May it shine brilliantly to the ends of the world.

Today, declare God's glory!

PSALM 25
////////////////////

to be guided

To you, O Lord, I lift up my soul.
O my God, in you I trust;
do not let me be put to shame;
do not let my enemies exult over me.
Do not let those who wait for you be put to shame;
let them be ashamed who are wantonly treacherous.

Make me to know your ways, O Lord;
teach me your paths.
Lead me in your truth, and teach me,
for you are the God of my salvation;
for you I wait all day long.

Be mindful of your mercy, O Lord, and of your steadfast love,
for they have been from of old.
Do not remember the sins of my youth or my transgressions;
according to your steadfast love remember me,
for your goodness' sake, O Lord!

Psalm 25:1–7

One day a pilot returned his plane to the mechanic's shop with this complaint, "Unfamiliar noise in engine." The next day the plane was back in service. The pilot checked the logbook to see what problem had been found. The entry read, "Ran engine continuously for four hours. Noise is now familiar."

What familiar noise is quietly dulling your excitement, ideas, or vision of life?

Sometimes we try to create personal, communal, or national boundaries to protect ourselves and control the unfamiliar. The psalmist reminds us that we have nothing to fear if we are walking on the path the Lord sets out for us.

The Guide and the guided. It is easy to confuse which is God and which is ourselves; easier still to allow distracting noise to become familiar.

The psalmist reminds us that God is the one in whom we are to trust, not ourselves.

> God our guide, keep me attentive to your voice.
> Lead me on your paths—passionate and daring.
> Guide me in your goodness. Guide me and
> teach me your ways.

Today, break a comfortable routine.
Try something new.

///////////////////

to speak peace

The voice of the LORD is over the waters;
the God of glory thunders,
the LORD, over mighty waters.
The voice of the LORD is powerful;
the voice of the LORD is full of majesty.

The voice of the LORD breaks the cedars;
the LORD breaks the cedars of Lebanon.
He makes Lebanon skip like a calf,
and Sirion like a young wild ox.

The voice of the LORD flashes forth flames of fire.
The voice of the LORD shakes the wilderness;
the LORD shakes the wilderness of Kadesh.

The voice of the LORD causes the oaks to whirl,
and strips the forest bare;
and in his temple all say, "Glory!"

The LORD sits enthroned over the flood;
the LORD sits enthroned as king forever.
May the LORD give strength to his people!
May the LORD bless his people with peace!

PSALM 29:3–11

Anne's illness had moved quickly throughout her body. The realization came with a shock of profound sadness, and her life changed instantly. She was no longer able to communicate with her friends throughout the nation, so her friend Julie began to call them and tell them of Anne's condition. She promised to keep everyone connected. She promised to carry their messages of love and prayers back to Anne.

Julie maintained these friendships for two weeks. They knew her only as "Anne's friend." Through Anne's last days of life, her vigil, and her funeral, Julie's voice carried precious descriptions to those who were unable to be present. In the days and emptiness following Anne's death, Julie knew there was one more thing she wanted to do for her friend.

In the Native American tradition of a "give away," Julie packed up special quilts, prayer blankets, and art work that had belonged to Anne. Then she traveled to meet the women who had become her telephone friends. She wanted to see their faces, hear their stories, and bring them a gift with which to remember their common friend.

She brought peace to Anne's sacred circle, who now welcomed her.

God of peace, your voice is powerful and full of majesty, but my heart is fragile right now. Speak to me in the glory of gentle strength. Speak to me, and bring to my heart your peace.

Today, call someone with whom you have lost touch.

to trust

Do not fret because of the wicked;
do not be envious of wrongdoers,
for they will soon fade like the grass,
and wither like the green herb.

Trust in the LORD, and do good;
so you will live in the land, and enjoy security.
Take delight in the LORD,
and he will give you the desires of your heart.

Commit your way to the LORD;
trust in him, and he will act.
He will make your vindication shine like the light,
and the justice of your cause like the noonday.

Be still before the LORD, and wait patiently for him;
do not fret over those who prosper in their way,
over those who carry out evil devices.

Refrain from anger, and forsake wrath.
Do not fret—it leads only to evil.
For the wicked shall be cut off,
but those who wait for the LORD shall inherit the land.

PSALM 37:1–9

One day an art professor's four-year-old daughter asked what he did at school. "I teach the students how to draw," said the father.

"You mean they *forget*?" asked the young girl, her eyes wide in amazement.

It's so easy to forget—how to draw, how to create, how to play. It's easy to forget that such activities came so naturally to us when we were young.

It's so easy to forget that if we trust in the Lord, he will act; that if we find our delight in the Lord, he will give us the desires of our heart. It's easy to forget all God promises us, because there is so much that can get in the way—envy, anger, impatience.

It's hard to even imagine that we are God's chosen ones.

We think, "Surely God is smarter than that!"

And that's the story we need to remember; it's not about us. It's about God.

So even if we have somehow "forgotten" God, it's not too late. God has not forgotten us.

Divine Artist, there are times I become so focused on myself that I forget life is about you. Remind me that you are my creator and that I am your masterpiece.

Today, paint or draw your prayer.

to thirst

As a deer longs for flowing streams,
so my soul longs for you, O God.
My soul thirsts for God,
for the living God.
When shall I come and behold
the face of God?
My tears have been my food
day and night,
while people say to me continually,
"Where is your God?"

These things I remember,
as I pour out my soul:
how I went with the throng,
and led them in procession to the house of God,
with glad shouts and songs of thanksgiving,
a multitude keeping festival.
Why are you cast down, O my soul,
and why are you disquieted within me?
Hope in God; for I shall again praise him,
my help and my God.

PSALM 42:1–6

The health-care worker could do nothing for the little girl in her arms but hold her and pray the milk would bring her sustenance. After a year of life, the imprint of the little one's body upon the Earth was still less than ten pounds. The imprint she left on the hearts of those who tried to save her life was beyond measure.

Her malnourished mother had been unable to nurse little Angelina Marie. Then the water they had used to mix the meager supply of formula became contaminated by waste from the sewage. Poverty made it impossible for the family to get medical help. In the end, they were forced to watch the horror of their daughter dying before their eyes.

The health-care worker could do nothing when she arrived with her simple nutrition assistance but hold Angelina Marie, offer her a bottle from which to drink, and pray.

> **Nurturing God, I thirst for you in silence when I am overpowered by noise. I thirst for you in gentleness when I am hardened by violence.**
> **I thirst for you in peace when I am tormented by doubts. I thirst.**

Today, savor a glass of fresh, cool water.
Pray for those who thirst.

PSALM 46

///////////////////

to call out

God is our refuge and strength,
a very present help in trouble.

Therefore we will not fear, though the earth should change,
though the mountains shake in the heart of the sea;
though its waters roar and foam,
though the mountains tremble with its tumult.

There is a river whose streams make glad the city of God,
the holy habitation of the Most High.
God is in the midst of the city; it shall not be moved;
God will help it when the morning dawns.

The nations are in an uproar, the kingdoms totter;
he utters his voice, the earth melts.

The LORD of hosts is with us;
the God of Jacob is our refuge

PSALM 46:1–7

She was recognized as a faithful mother, grandmother, and church member. So much so that many thought of her only as "Call Betty."

Betty was Mike's secretary for more than 25 years and throughout the course of three different careers. When they were young, Mike's children knew that if their parents were ever hurt in an accident, they were simply to "Call Betty."

When a person came to the office in confusion, anger, or any of a number of complicated problems, the front desk would say, "Call Betty." People in the area knew Betty would be able to organize an event, calm a conflict, and take care of a problem. She seemed to be able to handle any situation.

We can be still despite a multitude of challenges if we know who to call on in distress. Our strength alone is not always enough to meet the demands of the day. We can "call on God," who is our refuge and strength.

We can "call on God," who is our ever-present help in distress.

We can "call on God," whose voice melts all that is rigid or violent in our lives.

God, my ever-present help, I call on you. My world seems to be falling apart and I can no longer manage it all on my own. Let this time of distress teach me that I am not meant to carry it alone. Teach me to rely on your strength.

Today, write a note of thanks to a "Betty" in your life.

PSALM 48

to ponder

We ponder your steadfast love, O God,
in the midst of your temple.
Your name, O God, like your praise,
reaches to the ends of the earth.
Your right hand is filled with victory.
Let Mount Zion be glad,
let the towns of Judah rejoice
because of your judgments.

Walk about Zion, go all around it,
count its towers,
consider well its ramparts;
go through its citadels,
that you may tell the next generation
that this is God,
our God forever and ever.
He will be our guide forever.

PSALM 48:9–14

I t might have seemed like he was simply a young boy playing with a railroad set on the basement floor, but it was much more for Aidan. While the rest of the family was seated comfortably in the living room upstairs, Aidan pondered as he played.

"Isn't it great, Aunt Kelli?" he said excitedly. "Just think, my grampa is your brother and Uncle Tom is your brother, so we're all related!

"Derek is Uncle Tom's son and he's graduating, so my mom and dad came up here. And you came up here. And cuz of all that, you and I are playing trains right now. It's like a miracle!"

What might seem to be a complicated coincidence is a miracle to those who see with the eyes of faith.

It's easy to miss the miracles in our lives; the "coincidence" of playing trains, surrounded by relatives.

It's easy to forget to ponder how God protects us, how God is our stronghold, our guide.

We can forget to rejoice with the next generation—until we are surrounded by the joy of trains on a basement floor, surrounded by relatives.

"This is our God forever and ever!"

> **Lord of hosts, slow me down so that I may ponder your magnificent world. Let me see your hand in each encounter, feel your breath in each gust of wind, and be amazed at the design of the city in which I live.**

Today, walk rather than ride to your destination.

PSALM 78
///////////////////

to teach

Give ear, O my people, to my teaching;
incline your ears to the words of my mouth.
I will open my mouth in a parable;
I will utter dark sayings from of old,
things that we have heard and known,
that our ancestors have told us.

We will not hide them from their children;
we will tell to the coming generation
the glorious deeds of the LORD, and his might,
and the wonders that he has done.

He established a decree in Jacob,
and appointed a law in Israel,
which he commanded our ancestors
to teach to their children;
that the next generation might know them,
the children yet unborn,
and rise up and tell them to their children,
so that they should set their hope in God,
and not forget the works of God,
but keep his commandments.

PSALM 78:1–7

Mary Sue had been active in her church for many years. When new information about Scripture or Church teaching was presented, she followed it with great interest. When summer Bible camps became a thing of the past, she invited others to establish a religious-education program at their own church. When youth ministry became popular, Mary Sue formed the first youth group in her area.

She was a woman of vision who dreamed, invited, and inspired others—all from the confines of her wheelchair. While others might do the manual work, Mary Sue brought everyone together with her energetic smile.

Although Mary Sue had to be carried down stairways at times, she was never weighed down by her infirmities. She faced a declining population in her rural town, the closing of her local school, and the inattentiveness of generations of students. Yet she always found a way to breathe life into dry bones.

"The vision!" she would say. "We have to keep the vision of a church alive and singing. God is bigger than any and all of us!"

Divine Teacher, forgive me for when I have been reluctant to rise up and speak your message to the next generation. Inspire me to proclaim your glorious deeds. Breathe your passion into my words.

Today, tell someone about who has inspired you.

PSALM 86
//////////////////

to seek wisdom

Teach me your way, O LORD,
that I may walk in your truth;
give me an undivided heart to revere your name.
I give thanks to you, O Lord my God, with my whole heart,
and I will glorify your name forever.
For great is your steadfast love toward me;
you have delivered my soul from the depths of Sheol.

O God, the insolent rise up against me;
a band of ruffians seeks my life,
and they do not set you before them.
But you, O Lord, are a God merciful and gracious,
slow to anger and abounding in steadfast love and faithfulness.
Turn to me and be gracious to me;
give your strength to your servant;
save the child of your serving girl.
Show me a sign of your favor,
so that those who hate me may see it and be put to shame,
because you, LORD, have helped me and comforted me.

PSALM 86:11–17

Large circles of a different kind of grass are scattered about in the natural prairie pastures south of Barb's farm. A legend says these circles are where Native Americans set up their tepees. A different type of grass grew under the tepees. This type of grass is only present in the isolation of a vast prairie where there is no concrete for miles

For Barb, these circles offer a symbol of the continuity and sacredness of life. They offer a connection with the Native-American women who lived in these circles, cooked, cared for children, and created a home.

Barb brought her daughters here and shared the stories of her own life with them. She has brought women friends together to sit around a fire and celebrate an evening of storytelling. She has come here alone for her own inner survival.

Walking the path of the prairie circles allows Barb to reflect on a life lived before she was on this Earth.

Walking the path with her daughters and granddaughters allows Barb to share the stories that have shaped her life.

Walking the path allows Barb to live in truth.

Eternal Word, you have spoken in our hearts to all generations and to all nations. Teach me to listen deeply to the wisdom of the ages. Free me to share the stories of your faithfulness with those who come after me in your sacred circle of life.

Today, seek out an older person of wisdom.
Ask to hear stories of a past generation.

///////////////////

to grow old

Lord, you have been our dwelling place
in all generations.
Before the mountains were brought forth,
or ever you had formed the earth and the world,
from everlasting to everlasting you are God.

You turn us back to dust,
and say, "Turn back, you mortals."
For a thousand years in your sight
are like yesterday when it is past,
or like a watch in the night.

You sweep them away; they are like a dream,
like grass that is renewed in the morning;
in the morning it flourishes and is renewed;
in the evening it fades and withers.

PSALM 90:1–6

One year Tim joined his parents and a service team of people ranging in age from 69 to 85.

Tim's dad and a group of the men built a house in record time. His mom and her friends fed malnourished infants and taught non-English–speaking children to dance the Hokey Pokey. Couples married 40 and 50 years partnered to serve food to the homeless and provide clothing and fresh vegetables to more than 250 mothers.

As a child, Tim had experienced his parents' care for his needs, but to watch them do the same thing for the poor in a foreign country just seemed to take it up a notch.

Time passes quickly, like a watch in the night. But the contributions we make to improve the lives of others will yield a legacy for generations to come.

God of all ages, the many moments before now have brought us to today. The moments to come, though we know not their number nor their reality, we know their fragile and unlimited potential. May we use today wisely.

Today, seek out a project you can do
with people of many ages.

PSALM 95

////////////////////////

to worship

O come, let us sing to the LORD*;*
let us make a joyful noise to the rock of our salvation!
Let us come into his presence with thanksgiving;
let us make a joyful noise to him with songs of praise!
For the LORD *is a great God,*
and a great King above all gods.
In his hand are the depths of the earth;
the heights of the mountains are his also.
The sea is his, for he made it,
and the dry land, which his hands have formed.

O come, let us worship and bow down,
let us kneel before the LORD*, our Maker!*
For he is our God,
and we are the people of his pasture,
and the sheep of his hand.

O that today you would listen to his voice!

PSALM 95:1–7

Ernesto spent time with his friend in the Ixcán jungles of northern Guatemala. The area was devastated by the Civil War in the mid 1980s. In some villages, 60 percent of the people were massacred. The people now live a life of extreme poverty and violence brought on by drug trafficking.

Ernesto and his friend were welcomed with a fresh chicken, coconut, or watermelon everywhere they went. When they tried to protest the extravagance of the gift, they were told:

"Today we are alive. We are together.
Who knows what tomorrow will bring?"

TODAY is the day to hear God's voice.
TODAY is the day to joyfully sing our psalms.
TODAY is the day to bow down in worship.

Who knows if we will even see tomorrow.

Extravagant God, you speak in the beauty and bounty of each moment. Forgive me for the times when I have missed your voice, for those times when I am caught up in plans for the future or regrets about the past. Remind me that this is your time.

Today, live as if this is the only moment you have.
What would you like to do most?
Do it!

PSALM 108

////////////////////

to be steadfast

My heart is steadfast, O God, my heart is steadfast;
I will sing and make melody.
Awake, my soul!
Awake, O harp and lyre!
I will awake the dawn.
I will give thanks to you, O Lord, *among the peoples,*
and I will sing praises to you among the nations.
For your steadfast love is higher than the heavens,
and your faithfulness reaches to the clouds.

Be exalted, O God, above the heavens,
and let your glory be over all the earth.
Give victory with your right hand, and answer me,
so that those whom you love may be rescued.

Psalm 108:1–6

Marge always rose earlier than anyone else in the household to get things done. She went to bed later too, because there were always more things to do.

She cared for her children tenderly and patiently, as she sewed clothing and mended blue jeans out of necessity, not as a fashion trend. Her station wagon hauled newspapers for delivery routes, equipment for sporting events, instruments for band practice, groceries for simple meals, and the most precious cargo of all—her children.

No one delighted in her children's successes more than Marge, and no one could comfort them better in their failures. Her heart was steadfast. Her faith was strong. There was always a song on her lips.

> Generous God, I am so grateful for those who have mothered, mentored, and even disciplined me without any desire for recognition. May I be steadfast in gratitude and do the same.

Today, write a letter of thanks to your mother or to someone who has been steadfast in their motherly love.

///////////////

to lead

Praise the LORD!
Happy are those who fear the LORD,
who greatly delight in his commandments.

Their descendants will be mighty in the land;
the generation of the upright will be blessed.
Wealth and riches are in their houses,
and their righteousness endures forever.
They rise in the darkness as a light for the upright;
they are gracious, merciful, and righteous.
It is well with those who deal generously and lend,
who conduct their affairs with justice.
For the righteous will never be moved;
they will be remembered forever.
They are not afraid of evil tidings;
their hearts are firm, secure in the LORD.
Their hearts are steady, they will not be afraid;
in the end they will look in triumph on their foes.
They have distributed freely, they have given to the poor;
their righteousness endures forever;
their horn is exalted in honor.

PSALM 112:1–9

The children were lined up for the annual school Christmas pageant. The youngest ones were the most excited. They were going to be the stars who led everyone to the newborn baby.

The angels, the shepherds, and the wise men were all going to follow the little stars to the manger. The first graders, the middle school children, and even the teachers were going to follow the preschoolers to their correct place on stage.

Four-year-old Dominick was going to be a star. He fidgeted from one foot to the other. He checked his white bed-sheet tunic and made sure his halo was at the perfect tilt. In his mind, he rehearsed the exact time he was to go on stage and the path he was to take with his group.

As the principal walked among the children with assurances and reminders, Dominick waved for her to lean in close and whispered into her ear, "I'm ready, Sister. I've been getting ready for this part all year. I'm going to lead the people to Jesus."

Happy are those who are ready for the greatest service of all.

Happy are those who will lead the people to Jesus.

> **Leader of nations, in the great moments and daily tasks of my service, may I lead in such a way that others find Jesus, your son. Prepare me so that I may be always ready.**

Today, who has led you to Jesus?
How did they show you the way?
Do likewise.

to be still

O LORD, *my heart is not lifted up,*
my eyes are not raised too high;
I do not occupy myself with things
too great and too marvelous for me.
But I have calmed and quieted my soul,
like a weaned child with its mother;
my soul is like the weaned child that is with me.

O Israel, hope in the LORD
from this time on and forevermore.

Although it was a Sunday afternoon, Diane was working frantically to meet her deadlines. Projects seemed to have piled up, and although she tried to work harder, longer, and even more efficiently, there seemed to be no end in sight. Her muscles were tight and beginning to ache. Her self-criticizing inner voice was taking on a momentum of its own. Her impatience with her loved ones was creating a lonely distance.

Recognizing that she was just about at breaking point, Diane got up from her desk and walked outside. A smile crossed her face as she looked up at the sky. There, silhouetted against the white clouds and blue horizon, danced a red serpent kite. A little child and his mother were holding onto the string that kept the kite grounded to Earth.

Diane nestled deep into the prairie grass and watched the mother and child. She grieved her own mother and memories of sharing just this type of play.

Diane knew the work on her desk would wait another day. It was not the central work of her life. She took out her phone and called home.

Heavenly Father, forgive me when I act like
I am responsible for the whole world.
Help me to remember that you are God
and I am your beloved child.

Today, go fly a kite.

LIVING IN HOPE

Upon you I have leaned from my birth;
it was you who took me from my mother's womb.

PSALM 71:6

LIVING IN HOPE frees the soul from expectations of perfection that hold together a fragile, frightened, anxious self. It is knowing that life does not rely solely on our own efforts. Hope brings us face to face with the One who holds all things in his hands, our God.

It is upon God, not our own strength, that we lean. It is from God, not our own success or failure, that we draw our self-worth. With the psalmist, we are moved with pity, lifted up in our woundedness, given the courage to break into song. Tears flow forth, softening the dried-out and hardened heart, making it receptive to the truth.

In God, we realize the truth of how short we fall and how greatly we are loved—just as we are.

As if our attempts of enormous expectation are not enough for us, we often try to serve as little messiahs for others. We might not mean to, we might not notice—but we take on the responsibility for someone else's life. In doing so, we take away that person's responsibility and the way in which God might work in his or her life.

Living in hope allows us to become men and women of hospitality. We trust in the God who cares enough to let us live our own lives—in him—who cares for us all.

With the psalmist, people of hope sing of the elegance and messiness, the success and failure, the giftedness and neediness of the human adventure, welcoming the oneness we share with those with whom we walk.

Living in hope does not disregard pain or disappointment—it leans into it—as hope transforms, resurrects, and shows us the power of God. The God who took us from our mother's womb is with us now, always—forever.

PSALM 6

//////////////

to be healed

Be gracious to me, O LORD, for I am languishing;
O LORD, heal me, for my bones are shaking with terror.
My soul also is struck with terror,
while you, O LORD—how long?

Turn, O LORD, save my life;
deliver me for the sake of your steadfast love.
For in death there is no remembrance of you;
in Sheol who can give you praise?

I am weary with my moaning;
every night I flood my bed with tears;
I drench my couch with my weeping.
My eyes waste away because of grief;
they grow weak because of all my foes.

Depart from me, all you workers of evil,
for the LORD has heard the sound of my weeping.

PSALM 6:2–8

As Madison was brought to the door of the homeless shelter, some of the other girls immediately stepped back. She smelled, she obviously had lice, and her clothes hung on her defeated body. Her mother had gone out for the night and had not returned. It was a frequent occurrence in Madison's twelve years of life, but this time her mother had not returned after several days.

Madison was noticeably shuddering and weary with sighing. Her eyes were dim with sorrow that showed suffering beyond what a person twice her age should have known. *How long,* she wondered, *how long will I feel so alone and abandoned?*

Moved by pity, the woman at the door embraced Madison and welcomed her.

Moved by pity, Jesus embraced Peter's mother-in-law and raised her to life.

Moved by pity, Francis of Assisi embraced the person with leprosy and they were both healed.

Moved by pity, to whom are we called to go?

Healing God, I am filled with deep pain and brokenness. Bring my weary sighing back to life with your healing touch. Heal me so that I may be a channel of your compassion to others.

Today, let yourself be moved by pity.
What will you do?

to seek truth

Help, O LORD, for there is no longer anyone who is godly;
the faithful have disappeared from humankind.
They utter lies to each other;
with flattering lips and a double heart they speak.

May the LORD cut off all flattering lips,
the tongue that makes great boasts,
those who say, "With our tongues we will prevail;
our lips are our own—who is our master?"

"Because the poor are despoiled, because the needy groan,
I will now rise up," says the LORD;
"I will place them in the safety for which they long."
The promises of the LORD are promises that are pure,
silver refined in a furnace on the ground,
purified seven times.

You, O LORD, will protect us;
you will guard us from this generation forever.
On every side the wicked prowl,
as vileness is exalted among humankind.

The temperature had been dangerously cold for several days when Nick saw the middle-aged man sitting by the tree. He was definitely homeless, had definitely spent the night outside, and was possibly no longer alive. Nick approached him with caution to confirm that he was indeed alive under the blanket and asked if he could help.

The man was startled and frightened, then he quietly acknowledged that his feet were frozen. Nick helped him to stand, took him into a store lobby, and got him some coffee. Then he asked if he could call someone who would be able to help. The homeless man refused immediately, saying he had to keep moving.

Nick gathered some food and warm clothing, then gave him money for bus fare so he could continue his travel. He knew he was taking a risk, but Nick put forward his hand and said, "Let us speak truthfully and shake on it. I promise not to call anyone and report you, but I want you to promise not to harm me if I give you a ride to the bus station."

They spoke the truth. They shook hands.

They kept their promises.

God of truth, our world is so full of suspicion and betrayal. Help me to trust others. Teach me to speak simply and truthfully.

Today, purchase a gift certificate from a local fast-food restaurant. Give it to the next person you see who looks like he or she might need it.

PSALM 20

to shout with joy

The LORD answer you in the day of trouble!
The name of the God of Jacob protect you!
May he send you help from the sanctuary,
and give you support from Zion.
May he remember all your offerings,
and regard with favor your burnt sacrifices.

May he grant you your heart's desire,
and fulfill all your plans.
May we shout for joy over your victory,
and in the name of our God set up our banners.
May the LORD fulfill all your petitions.

Now I know that the LORD will help his anointed;
he will answer him from his holy heaven
with mighty victories by his right hand.
Some take pride in chariots, and some in horses,
but our pride is in the name of the LORD our God.
They will collapse and fall,
but we shall rise and stand upright.

Give victory to the king, O LORD;
answer us when we call.

They straggled in—nine men in gray prison garb—and began their first class on "Exploring Christianity." Robert and Art had been raised in active faith families, but this was Donzel's first exposure to religion.

His life on the streets had imprinted an understanding of churches as a warm escape from the cold where kind people served him food and temporary "basement housing." Donzel had never ventured to climb the massive steps to the actual worship space. He had never felt worthy to take part in the worshiping community.

At one point during the class, Donzel literally jumped out of his seat and declared, "Man, I'm glad I'm learning this stuff now. I can't imagine not having God on my side."

Some rely on chariots, others on horses.

Some rely on intellect, others on self-righteousness.

Donzel and the men in prison know it is only in the Lord that they will be saved. They had tried other pathways, but life had collapsed and fallen for them. Now they can't imagine not having God on their side.

> Saving God, renew within me the wholehearted amazement of your saving power in my life. Let me shout for joy. Let me cry in gratitude. Let me walk every step of every day with you at my side.

Today, listen to a Christian radio station and let the music move you. What do the songs say about God?

PSALM 22
///////////////////

to cry for help

My God, my God, why have you forsaken me?
Why are you so far from helping me, from the words of my
    groaning?
O my God, I cry by day, but you do not answer;
and by night, but find no rest.

Yet you are holy,
enthroned on the praises of Israel.
In you our ancestors trusted;
they trusted, and you delivered them.
To you they cried, and were saved;
in you they trusted, and were not put to shame.

But I am a worm, and not human;
scorned by others, and despised by the people.
All who see me mock at me;
they make mouths at me, they shake their heads;
"Commit your cause to the Lord; let him deliver—
let him rescue the one in whom he delights!"

PSALM 22:1–8

t's a nonnegotiable," Maggie cried out to her friend. "Jack can't die. I won't let it happen."

Maggie was used to relying on her strong intellect to solve problems. She had been a champion debater in school. She knew how to build consensus. She had run political campaigns, instituted educational programs, and believed in her ability to make change happen—especially when she cared about something—and she cared fiercely about Jack.

What Maggie needed to learn could only be found in surrendering herself to the anguish and loss that Jack's illness and impending death would mean for her.

She learned that prayer was not an act of persuading God, but one of entrusting her needs to God with total abandonment.

Life was not an intellectual exercise to be mastered, but a fragile mystery to be cherished.

Strength was not to be found in battling everything alone, but in crying out to the One who hears our anguish and pain.

Saving God, I am powerless and want to run from the pain. Calm my fear. Gentle my anger. Heal my need to always be in control. Hold me close to your heart.

Today, take a walk in a cemetery. Reflect on your own mortality.

PSALM 30
/////////////////////

to comfort

I will extol you, O LORD, for you have drawn me up,
and did not let my foes rejoice over me.
O LORD my God, I cried to you for help,
and you have healed me.
O LORD, you brought up my soul from Sheol,
restored me to life from among those gone down to the Pit.

Sing praises to the LORD, O you his faithful ones,
and give thanks to his holy name.
For his anger is but for a moment;
his favor is for a lifetime.
Weeping may linger for the night,
but joy comes with the morning.

PSALM 30:1–5

t had been a long week in the waiting room at the cancer center. The initial tears had seemed to pass and the inevitable diagnosis accepted. The family members had been notified to come home, but everyone was still waiting to hear from Jean.

As the family moved sorrowfully down the hallway toward the cafeteria, Jill's phone rang. "It's Jean!" she exclaimed, and everyone gathered around. Jean's voice brought completeness to the circle of family. Even at a distance, her soothing personality and prayerful words brought comfort to her exhausted sisters. "It's Jean!" they said to one another, and the tears began to flow once again.

Just at that moment, a member of the housekeeping staff was making her way down the hallway with a cart of supplies. Reverencing the sacredness of the family's grief, the woman simply reached into her cart and brought out a box of tissues. She handed it to one of the sisters with a soft touch of her hand that said, "I understand," then moved on down the hallway.

God of comfort, I yearn for the touch of kindness in the harshness of this world. I yearn for a voice of connection in the ache of this loneliness. I yearn for the promised joy of morning in this nighttime of tears. I yearn for you.

Today, show extra kindness to those who serve you in the restaurant, grocery store, office, or school.

PSALM 31

/////////////////////////

to take heart

In you, O LORD, I seek refuge;
do not let me ever be put to shame;
in your righteousness deliver me.
Incline your ear to me;
rescue me speedily.
Be a rock of refuge for me,
a strong fortress to save me.
You are indeed my rock and my fortress;
for your name's sake lead me and guide me,
take me out of the net that is hidden for me,
for you are my refuge.
Into your hand I commit my spirit;
you have redeemed me, O LORD, faithful God.

You hate those who pay regard to worthless idols,
but I trust in the LORD.
I will exult and rejoice in your steadfast love,
because you have seen my affliction;
you have taken heed of my adversities,
and have not delivered me into the hand of the enemy;
you have set my feet in a broad place.

PSALM 31:1–8

saac met Jim on the Friday morning of his discharge. Jim came out of the prison with only his backpack and a mesh laundry bag of clothing. They drove to the bank so Jim could cash the check for money he had saved from his 75-cent-an-hour job at the prison. They drove to the rundown hotel that catered to ex-felons, registered sex offenders, transients, and others who could find no better options.

They reported in with his parole officer, then went to the social-services office so Jim could register for food stamps and acquire some staples from the food pantry.

If Isaac had not met Jim at the prison gates, Jim would have navigated these trips alone and on foot. The seemingly simple tasks would have been far more overwhelming for this older man coming from six years in an institution. His sentence had been completed, but he felt the shame of his crime so deeply that he thought it was visible to all.

Isaac was a stronghold for Jim as he stayed at his side. He was a bestower for his needs and, most important, a protector of his fragile heart.

Renewer of hearts, surrounded by fear and anxiety, I take refuge in you. Send a holy angel to be my companion as I walk unfamiliar paths. Speak words of healing and forgiveness as I strive to be faithful. Set my feet in a free and open space that I may celebrate your love.

Today, forgive yourself.

to savor the lord

O taste and see that the LORD is good;
happy are those who take refuge in him.
O fear the LORD, you his holy ones,
for those who fear him have no want.
The young lions suffer want and hunger,
but those who seek the LORD lack no good thing.

Come, O children, listen to me;
I will teach you the fear of the LORD.
Which of you desires life,
and covets many days to enjoy good?
Keep your tongue from evil,
and your lips from speaking deceit.
Depart from evil, and do good;
seek peace, and pursue it.

The eyes of the LORD are on the righteous,
and his ears are open to their cry.

PSALM 34:8–15

t was an unseasonably hot day. It seemed like everyone was looking for some kind of relief, so an ice cream store was a natural place to stop.

Shannon clutched her money tightly and stood at the entrance to the store. She read the sign that said, "No bare feet." She looked at her toes wiggling free and sadly turned to leave, just as Paul was coming out of the store.

He watched as she walked away and then called out to her. As Shannon made her way back, Paul sat down on the curb, took off his size 12 shoes, and set them in front of her, saying, "Here, you won't be able to walk far, but if you slide along, you can get to the ice cream counter."

Paul lifted the little girl and set her feet into his shoes. "Take your time," he said. "It'll feel good for me to just sit here and enjoy my ice cream cone." Her eyes shone with a joy that couldn't be missed as Shannon shuffled up to the counter and ordered her cone.

Paul was a big man. Big belly, big shoes, but most of all, he had a big heart.

Gracious God, I delight in the many gifts that flow day and night into my life. Attune me to your many blessings. Invite me to walk in your goodness—in your shoes. Teach me to live with a bigness of heart.

Today, savor the taste of your food.

///////////////

to seek God

O Lord, all my longing is known to you;
my sighing is not hidden from you.
My heart throbs, my strength fails me;
as for the light of my eyes—it also has gone from me.
My friends and companions stand aloof from my affliction,
and my neighbors stand far off.

Those who seek my life lay their snares;
those who seek to hurt me speak of ruin,
and meditate treachery all day long.

But I am like the deaf, I do not hear;
like the mute, who cannot speak.
Truly, I am like one who does not hear,
and in whose mouth is no retort.

But it is for you, O LORD, that I wait;
it is you, O LORD my God, who will answer.

PSALM 38:9–15

than saw the other baby and took off with all the speed he could muster. He crawled across the carpet toward his new friend and crawled right into the full-length mirror!

Startled at this abrupt stop, Ethan looked puzzled at the baby staring back at him, who was equally startled. His slightly older brother, Andy, looked around at the family and laughed at his baby brother's antics in front of the mirror.

Longing for a friend, the baby went after a reflection of himself.

Longing for the Lord, adults often create gods as a reflection of themselves. We bump and are startled when it is not the real thing.

But the Lord knows.

The Lord will answer.

> **Come, O come, Emmanuel, and free me from my preoccupation with self. Broaden my worldview to care for those who are different from me. Deepen my motivation to seek you above all else.**

Today, whenever you pass a mirror, pray,
"Come, Lord, come into my life."

to awaken the dawn

My heart is steadfast, O God,
my heart is steadfast.
I will sing and make melody.
Awake, my soul!
Awake, O harp and lyre!
I will awake the dawn.
I will give thanks to you, O Lord, among the peoples;
I will sing praises to you among the nations.
For your steadfast love is as high as the heavens;
your faithfulness extends to the clouds.

Be exalted, O God, above the heavens.
Let your glory be over all the earth.

PSALM 57:7–11

Amid their busy life with seven children, Jordan's mom and dad would periodically travel "by themselves." A lot of times, it was connected to a business-oriented convention, but it was time together. Over the years, certain traditions arose around these trips.

The boys would take responsibility for the yard; the girls kept the house clean. The grandmothers would take turns staying with the family. And on every trip, regardless of the length, Jordan's parents would send a postcard home, a different one for each child.

When the children grew up and were on their own, they still received postcards. The trips lengthened. The grandmothers were no longer there. The children each had their own home. Yet, through all the years, the message basically stayed the same, "Thinking about you. Love you. It's a magnificent world, keep exploring it."

Every dawn is a postcard from God.

Dazzling in beauty, exhilarating in possibility.

The message basically stays the same, "Thinking about you. Love you. It's a magnificent world, keep exploring it."

Lord of the universe, I awaken to join all creation in a song of praise to you. I exalt in the many ways you will reveal yourself to me this day. May I live these hours with gratitude, with a spirit of humble service, and with an explorer's zest.

Today, send a postcard.

to extend blessing

May God be gracious to us and bless us
and make his face to shine upon us,
that your way may be known upon earth,
your saving power among all nations.
Let the peoples praise you, O God;
let all the peoples praise you.

Let the nations be glad and sing for joy,
for you judge the peoples with equity
and guide the nations upon earth.
Let the peoples praise you, O God;
let all the peoples praise you.

The earth has yielded its increase;
God, our God, has blessed us.
May God continue to bless us;
let all the ends of the earth revere him.

Marcia was born in Antigua, Guatemala, in 1982. Over the next several years, she drew the same heart-and-bird pictures with colored pencils held in her toes, a begging basket in her wheelchair. Marcia had a smile and a kind word for all the people on the street. Tourist or tramp—she treated them all with dignity.

One morning a handwritten sign appeared on the chair where Marcia had grown from a young girl to a woman. It simply read, "May 7, 2010. Marcia died." The basket remained to receive donations to buy this beautiful woman a final resting place from which her heart and body would be free to fly.

Marcia's disability did not define her any more than the poverty in which she survived.

Marcia was defined by the radiance of her face and the gentleness of her voice. She was known for the vibrancy of her colors and the simplicity of her drawings.

Marcia was blessing. And people from all nations praised God because they had been in her presence.

> May God be gracious and bless us. May I live this day in such a way that others are more joyful, more gentle, and more kind because we have shared a moment together.
> May God be praised in my living.

Today, say "God bless you" to others and mean it.

//////////////

to hope

In you, O LORD, I take refuge;
let me never be put to shame.
In your righteousness deliver me and rescue me;
incline your ear to me and save me.
Be to me a rock of refuge,
a strong fortress, to save me,
for you are my rock and my fortress.

Rescue me, O my God, from the hand of the wicked,
from the grasp of the unjust and cruel.
For you, O Lord, are my hope,
my trust, O LORD, from my youth.

Upon you I have leaned from my birth;
it was you who took me from my mother's womb.
My praise is continually of you.

PSALM 71:1–6

Craig had been walking in the Italian heat for hours when he heard the music. It absolutely mesmerized him. The sound of a single violin seemed to fill the piazza as it floated over the crowd. The music touched the place in his heart where he was tired of being a tourist and where he was feeling lost in the mass of people. His search for the source of the music gave him a renewed energy to keep pressing through the crowd.

He climbed the stairway, hurried through the church piazza, and sped past the rich marble façade and the exquisite mosaics of the Gothic cathedral. They would all be there on his return. For now, he had just one goal: the music and the musician.

When he found the source of the music, Craig was surprised but not disappointed. Milan was a peasant from the Czech Republic and sat under a tree in a back courtyard, away from the crowds. He had not set out a basket for donations, nor did he have recordings for sale.

Milan was playing his violin simply because at that moment he felt an overwhelming passion for life.

That is what Craig heard over the noise of the crowd.

That is what Craig desired more than anything.

God of all hope, rescue me from simply living as part of the crowd. Play a melody that inspires me to search for you. Fill my heart with a longing that can only be fulfilled in you. Call me to a life of passion and hope.

Today, listen to a hauntingly beautiful piece of music.

to break into song

O sing to the LORD a new song,
for he has done marvelous things.
His right hand and his holy arm
have gotten him victory.
The LORD has made known his victory;
he has revealed his vindication in the sight of the nations.
He has remembered his steadfast love and faithfulness
to the house of Israel.
All the ends of the earth have seen
the victory of our God.

Make a joyful noise to the LORD, all the earth;
break forth into joyous song and sing praises.
Sing praises to the LORD with the lyre,
with the lyre and the sound of melody.
With trumpets and the sound of the horn
make a joyful noise before the King, the LORD.

Let the sea roar, and all that fills it;
the world and those who live in it.
Let the floods clap their hands;
let the hills sing together for joy
at the presence of the LORD, for he is coming
to judge the earth.
He will judge the world with righteousness,
and the peoples with equity.

The Christian musician brought energy, song, and a full-bodied laugh to the stage. At one point, he invited the children to join him. Hanna had been transfixed from the moment he had walked into the room, so she quickly darted up. She sang and danced, filling the entire auditorium with her enthusiasm. Upon returning to her grandmother, Hanna declared with all of her five-year-old wisdom, *"This* is the greatest moment of my *entire* life!"

That's all we've got, isn't it? Just this moment. This moment in which the Lord is doing marvelous things. This moment in which the Lord is making his victory known in the sight of all.

Let us respond with childlike enthusiasm and join all creation in a dance of joy. Bring out the trumpets and horns, the kazoos and maracas, the homemade instruments of younger days. Break into songs of delight and amazement, for our God is with us. Our God is victorious. Our God is jubilantly inviting us to be his dance partner. *Now* is indeed the greatest moment!

> Jubilant God, every cell within my body vibrates with energy. The crispness of morning air, the grandeur of mountain height, the rhythm of river and sea call to me. I enter the dance of life with you as my partner.

Today, skip, dance, burst into song.

////////////////////////

to bless the lord

Bless the Lord, *O my soul,*
and all that is within me,
bless his holy name.

Bless the Lord, *O my soul,*
and do not forget all his benefits—
who forgives all your iniquity,
who heals all your diseases,
who redeems your life from the Pit,
who crowns you with steadfast love and mercy,
who satisfies you with good as long as you live
so that your youth is renewed like the eagle's.

Psalm 103:1–5

Susan gently touched the African violet, leaned in and whispered, "Grow, beautiful plant. Become strong and green. Bring forth flowers for our home."

Each day Susan would walk down the hallway and with the same tender voice sing, "Good morning. Have a wonderful day." She would pray for people in her community and in her family, asking God to help them grow into the persons God most dreamed they could become.

To be near Susan was to feel renewed like the eagle.

It was to believe you were capable of growth and beauty.

It was to open your eyes to the good things of life.

To be near Susan was to remember that, above all, you were a gift of God. Tenderly nurtured. Surrounded with love. Pardoned of all your sins.

Blessed.

Bless the Lord, my soul, and let me speak words of blessing to all those I meet this day.
May my words be gentle, merciful, and compassionate. May my words bring life and beauty. May my words truly be of God.

Today, nurture a plant and whisper to it,
"Grow strong and beautiful."
Imagine God tenderly whispering
the same to you.

/////////////////////

to take delight

With my whole heart I seek you;
do not let me stray from your commandments.
I treasure your word in my heart,
so that I may not sin against you.
Blessed are you, O LORD;
teach me your statutes.
With my lips I declare
all the ordinances of your mouth.
I delight in the way of your decrees
as much as in all riches.
I will meditate on your precepts,
and fix my eyes on your ways.
I will delight in your statutes;
I will not forget your word.

PSALM 119:10–16

The small faith community was engaged in a lively discussion about favorite books. Sister Norma, at age 97, was a devoted reader, but that night she was grasping for the name of an author. When the conversation settled down to prayer, the group began with prayers of thanksgiving.

As different members offered prayers of thanksgiving for the blessings of their lives, Sister Norma began, "I thank God that I remembered the name of that author is John Grisham." With a twinkle in her eye, she then looked at the group and added, "I also thank God that he cares about the little things in our lives as well as the important."

The group paused and recognized the profound truth in her humorous comment.

That's the way it is between people deeply in love. Nothing is trivial or unimportant. The word of the beloved is a treasure; the way of the beloved brings delight.

Beloved Friend, speak to me in the events of this day, no matter how trivial. May I delight in the surprises you place within each task, encounter, and moment of rest.

Today, take delight in one of the "trivial" tasks of your day, such as washing the dishes or making your bed.

//////////////////////

to laugh

When the Lord restored the fortunes of Zion,
we were like those who dream.
Then our mouth was filled with laughter,
and our tongue with shouts of joy;
then it was said among the nations,
"The Lord has done great things for them."
The Lord has done great things for us,
and we rejoiced.

Restore our fortunes, O Lord,
like the watercourses in the Negeb.
May those who sow in tears
reap with shouts of joy.
Those who go out weeping,
bearing the seed for sowing,
shall come home with shouts of joy,
carrying their sheaves.

Josh had prepared for the grand opening of his new shop, and everything was perfect. The guest list and invitations had the ideal balance of civic, professional, and personal attendees. The food was tasteful, decorations distinctive, and the flowers would soon be arriving.

When they did arrive, however, Josh was aghast. There on the large centerpiece bouquet was a ribbon declaring, "Rest in peace."

He called the florist in a panic. Her calming tone held a chuckle as she placed Josh's predicament in perspective.

"We will be able to get you a new ribbon for your flowers immediately. But while you wait, imagine the family gathering at a funeral home around their dearly deceased. They just received your bouquet decorated with a ribbon that says, 'Good luck in your new location.'"

> Gracious God, I rejoice that you are a God
> of laughter and tears, for my life holds both.
> Free me from inflated illusions of control and
> self-importance. Gift me with a trust in you
> that releases my tongue to sing for joy.

Today, learn a joke and
share it with three other people.

to wait

Out of the depths I cry to you, O LORD.
Lord, hear my voice!
Let your ears be attentive
to the voice of my supplications!

If you, O LORD, should mark iniquities,
Lord, who could stand?
But there is forgiveness with you,
so that you may be revered.

I wait for the LORD, my soul waits,
and in his word I hope;
my soul waits for the Lord
more than those who watch for the morning,
more than those who watch for the morning.

O Israel, hope in the LORD!
For with the LORD there is steadfast love,
and with him is great power to redeem.
It is he who will redeem Israel
from all its iniquities.

Kathryn loved to bake cookies for her friends. Though she didn't eat many herself, she found delight in sharing them with others. As she aged, she adjusted the recipes so that she was able to continue to share her delight and abundance.

Eventually, Kathryn became more unsteady, so much that she was unable to carry a pan of cookies across the kitchen. She became more forgetful, lost track of time and burned her delicacies. She did not, however, become any less generous, loving, or creative.

Kathryn would set a chair in front of the oven and watch the cookies bake. Peering in the little window, she frequently opened the door to confirm the light-gold coloring. Checking her watch and timer to be as certain as possible that she was not overbaking, she imagined the faces of delight the gift would bring.

As she watched and waited, Kathryn found time to include a prayer that blessings would accompany her offering.

God of Sabbath moments, each second of life is sacred; help me not wish it away. Free me from the addiction to speed and activity. Lead me into a gentle attentiveness that nurtures prayer and presence.

Today, while waiting in line, offer a prayer for the various people you see around you.

PSALM 142

to be free

With my voice I cry to the LORD;
with my voice I make supplication to the LORD.
I pour out my complaint before him;
I tell my trouble before him.
When my spirit is faint,
you know my way.

In the path where I walk
they have hidden a trap for me.
Look on my right hand and see—
there is no one who takes notice of me;
no refuge remains to me;
no one cares for me.

I cry to you, O LORD;
I say, "You are my refuge,
my portion in the land of the living."
Give heed to my cry,
for I am brought very low.

Save me from my persecutors,
for they are too strong for me.
Bring me out of prison,
so that I may give thanks to your name.
The righteous will surround me,
for you will deal bountifully with me.

Jacinta had dreams of visiting the United States and becoming a famous model. When a wealthy-looking man approached her in the marketplace and promised to introduce her to some important people who could make her dreams come true, Jacinta was thrilled.

She left her village, her family, and all that was familiar. She traveled with other girls who lived the same dream. Upon their arrival in the United States, their "benefactor" took their passports and made the promised introductions.

For the next several years, Jacinta endured nine to ten "customers" a night. Every night.

Unable to produce a passport, Jacinta feared being deported.

Unable to speak the language, Jacinta had no friend in whom to confide.

Unable to believe her family would accept her back, Jacinta became imprisoned in what she had hoped would be her dream.

Source of hope, hear the cry of your broken children, imprisoned in conditions beyond their strength. Save them from persecutors of mind, body, and spirit. Free them to return to those who love them. Challenge me to be a voice for the voiceless.

Today, research the number of children trafficked into the United States for sex every year. Pray for them.

PSALM 147
/////////////////

to bind up wounds

Praise the LORD!
How good it is to sing praises to our God;
for he is gracious, and a song of praise is fitting.

The LORD builds up Jerusalem;
he gathers the outcasts of Israel.
He heals the brokenhearted,
and binds up their wounds.

He determines the number of the stars;
he gives to all of them their names.
Great is our Lord, and abundant in power;
his understanding is beyond measure.
The LORD lifts up the downtrodden;
he casts the wicked to the ground.

PSALM 147:1–6

S he sat in the family visiting room of the state penitentiary, waiting for her father. People were drawn to her softness in that world of cold steel, and they smiled. The women especially couldn't help but smile as her little girl body cradled a doll, much like their own remembrances from so many years ago.

She rocked back and forth. She sang for only her dolly to hear. She sang this song:

"Sleep now, dear baby.
Daddy will come home someday
 and we will be happy.
Sleep now, dear baby,
 the hunger will go away.
We'll have a home someday
 and we will be happy."

It was a doll so much like they remembered, but a song she should never have needed to know.

Our God of power and wisdom holds close the vulnerable like this little one. He gives aid to the poor. He heals the brokenhearted. He binds up their wounds.

He expects no less from you and me.

Tender God, open my eyes to see the wounded around me. Open my ears to hear their song of pain and hope. Open my heart, my closet, my pocketbook, my schedule, to respond as your disciple.

Today, perform one act that will help the poor.

/////////////////////////

to give praise

Praise the LORD!
Praise God in his sanctuary;
praise him in his mighty firmament!
Praise him for his mighty deeds;
praise him according to his surpassing greatness!

Praise him with trumpet sound;
praise him with lute and harp!
Praise him with tambourine and dance;
praise him with strings and pipe!
Praise him with clanging cymbals;
praise him with loud clashing cymbals!
Let everything that breathes praise the LORD!
Praise the LORD!

Tammy never slept soundly when she went camping. Invariably, the family would set their tent in a location where a twig or stone would settle right into the middle of her back. The familiar sounds of her husband's sleep would take on a larger-than-life volume in the outdoors. She was always too warm or too cool in her sleeping bag, or there was a constant tussle between the extremes.

But Tammy spends every possible weekend enduring this type of insomnia for two reasons. The first is because she treasures the unplugged, unscheduled time with her family. The second reason is purely selfish: waking in the morning.

Crawling out from her tent, as a newborn from its mother's womb, Tammy stands on wobbly legs. It is as if she joins this little corner of the Earth in praising the Lord:

> Grasshopper song and cricket cry praise the Lord.
> Breath of wind and rustle of trees praise the Lord.
> Cascading stream and silent lake praise the Lord.

The laughter and bickering of children will soon interrupt Tammy's time of solitude. The cry of hunger and demands of motherhood will soon end her quiet sitting. May they, too, praise the Lord!

Marvelous Lord, free me to sing in harmony with all the Earth and all peoples. May I taste, touch, see, hear, and smell the wonders of creation as I go about my day. May I praise you in my busyness and rest. May I praise you in my words and silence. May everything that breathes praise you!

Today, sit in the beauty of the dawn.

//////////////

LIVING IN LOVE

//////////////

For it was you who formed my inward parts;
you knit me together in my mother's womb.

PSALM 139:13

L IVING IN LOVE is not easy. It is to become restless with
longing; to become seekers who must release the goal of the
search and allow ourselves to be found.

Living in love is to be vulnerable, intimately known by the One
who is our creator. With the psalmist, we plea, we cling, we beg
to be washed clean of all that gets in the way of complete union
with our Beloved.

We were created for union with God and will find fulfillment
only in that. We seek to find words to describe our desire, but we
can only do so by plunging into the abyss of silence or soaring
with the language of poets and artists. Such is the paradox of love.

As we come to know and be known by the living God, our
awareness of being loved unconditionally has a profound effect
on every relationship and everything we experience. When we are
living in love, we realize there are no strangers. We glimpse the
infinite preciousness of every person, animal, flower, mountain,
and stream in this amazing universe.

With the psalmist, we pray to be poured out in service, to live
in unity, to treasure and take pleasure in life. We feel life in all its
depths, in joy as well as sorrow.

//////////////

to treasure

Protect me, O God, for in you I take refuge.
I say to the LORD, "You are my Lord;
I have no good apart from you."

As for the holy ones in the land, they are the noble,
in whom is all my delight.

Those who choose another god multiply their sorrows;
their drink offerings of blood I will not pour out
or take their names upon my lips.

The LORD is my chosen portion and my cup;
you hold my lot.
The boundary lines have fallen for me in pleasant places;
I have a goodly heritage.

PSALM 16:1–6

W ould you like to say hi to Margaret?" always entered the conversation when Michael stopped to visit Dave. Margaret had Alzheimer's, and with the help of many faithful caregivers, Dave cared for her at home.

Today was no different. "Would you like to say hi to Margaret? She will be so glad you stopped." Michael followed Dave into her room, and Dave sat in his chair next to her bed. "Margaret," he began, "someone is here to see you."

Margaret lay there unresponsive as Michael greeted her. Dave sat at his wife's side, held her hand, and included her in the conversation. After a little time, Dave thanked Michael for visiting and walked him to the door with the familiar invitation to "Come again. Margaret loves company." Then Dave returned to his chair and his reading material—more than likely an economic report or trends in the oil business.

Dave was a wealthy man. His home was decorated with treasures from numerous trips abroad.

His real treasure, however, lay speechless in the bed in their room, dressed and ready for the next visitor.

God of life, you are the source and center of my being; all else is secondary. In my times of strength, humble me. In my times of weakness, protect me. You are my Lord; I have no good apart from you.

Today, visit a person who is homebound.

PSALM 17

//////////////

to plead

Hear a just cause, O LORD; attend to my cry;
give ear to my prayer from lips free of deceit.
From you let my vindication come;
let your eyes see the right.

If you try my heart, if you visit me by night,
if you test me, you will find no wickedness in me;
my mouth does not transgress.
As for what others do, by the word of your lips
I have avoided the ways of the violent.
My steps have held fast to your paths;
my feet have not slipped.

I call upon you, for you will answer me, O God;
incline your ear to me, hear my words.
Wondrously show your steadfast love,
O savior of those who seek refuge
from their adversaries at your right hand.

Guard me as the apple of the eye;
hide me in the shadow of your wings.

PSALM 17:1–8

The refrain of a popular country song kept going through Zachary's mind as he walked from the CEO's office. In the refrain the artist wishes not to know something now that he didn't know before.

Zachary wished he didn't know that just causes could get caught in the politics of power. He wished he didn't know that people could be so seemingly manipulative, cold, and detached. Zachary wished he didn't know that he could become so angry or despondent.

That was the plea Zachary felt most deeply in his heart. He really wished he could go on pretending that brokenness doesn't happen and that all is pleasant and nice. He did not want to enter the desert, but that was where he was called.

He understood the temptation of Jesus in the desert.

He understood Peter's denial.

He understood his own sinfulness.

And Zachary believed more deeply than ever that only in God was his refuge and his strength.

God of justice and mercy, guard me as the apple of your eye, and show me your strength and wisdom. Hide me in the shadow of your wings and renew my commitment to justice.

Have mercy, O God, in my need.

Have mercy on all your people.

Today, pray for victims of violence and for those who commit acts of violence.

PSALM 18
///////////////

to be protected

The cords of death encompassed me;
the torrents of perdition assailed me;
the cords of Sheol entangled me;
the snares of death confronted me.

In my distress I called upon the Lord;
to my God I cried for help.
From his temple he heard my voice,
and my cry to him reached his ears.

Then the earth reeled and rocked;
the foundations also of the mountains trembled
and quaked, because he was angry.
Smoke went up from his nostrils,
and devouring fire from his mouth;
glowing coals flamed forth from him.
He bowed the heavens, and came down;
thick darkness was under his feet.
He rode on a cherub, and flew;
he came swiftly upon the wings of the wind.

PSALM 18:4–10

t was a familiar, simple ice breaker: "As a child, where did you go to feel safe?"

Cortez listened attentively to the others and reflected on the question for himself. Then, when it came to his turn, Cortez politely passed. Growing up in the projects of south Chicago, he just couldn't think of a time or place where he felt safe.

Standing in the aftermath of a tornado,
climbing through the debris left by a flood,
trembling with the aftershocks of an earthquake,
there are times we, too, feel utterly terrified and unsafe.

There is no logic to the devastation and no rationale to the path of destruction. Preventative measures are not able to stop the fury of the storm. At such times, we are encompassed in the snares of death but for the power of God.

God, who hears our cry and flares up with a protective love. God who knows that no human being alone can protect us right now.

Nothing can stop God from coming to our rescue. Nothing.

God, my protector, I am terrified and in distress. I can offer no polite, prayerful words, only the deep cry of anguish that arises unbidden. No, Gentle Shepherd, now I need your power and strength to protect me in this time of destruction.

Today, groan, shout, truly cry out to God.

to lack nothing

The LORD is my shepherd, I shall not want.
He makes me lie down in green pastures;
he leads me beside still waters;
he restores my soul.
He leads me in right paths
for his name's sake.

Even though I walk through the darkest valley,
I fear no evil;
for you are with me;
your rod and your staff—
they comfort me.

You prepare a table before me
in the presence of my enemies;
you anoint my head with oil;
my cup overflows.
Surely goodness and mercy shall follow me
all the days of my life,
and I shall dwell in the house of the LORD
my whole life long.

Maurice never thought it would happen to him, but here he was in the soup-kitchen line. He spoke to no one and kept his eyes cast to the ground as he accepted the tray of food from the cheery volunteer, grateful that his staunchly independent father was not alive to see his disgrace.

He sat down to eat and mumbled his thanks, then Maurice continued in silence until she came up behind him. "She" was a large, matronly woman with a booming laugh and a quick retort. As she approached, Maurice prepared himself for a joke but was caught off-guard when she spoke tenderly, "Son, you have cookies on your plate but no milk. Let me get you some cold milk; you deserve the best treatment tonight."

In her eyes, Maurice deserved the best, not the least.

He was treated with dignity, not blame.

He was offered milk to go with his cookies.

In that simple gesture, his cup was overflowing.

Shepherd of souls, I am mindful of my poverty and neediness. I surrender myself to your loving care, for you alone know the deepest longings of my heart. In you I lack nothing.

Today, be gentle.

PSALM 24

/////////////////

to know the lord

Lift up your heads, O gates!
and be lifted up, O ancient doors!
that the King of glory may come in.
Who is the King of glory?
The Lord, strong and mighty,
the Lord, mighty in battle.
Lift up your heads, O gates!
and be lifted up, O ancient doors!
that the King of glory may come in.
Who is this King of glory?
The Lord of hosts,
he is the King of glory.

Psalm 24:7–10

It was Palm Sunday, and Daneysha couldn't get the baby in her arms to stop crying. She had no milk for the bottle, no warm water for the bath. There was no one else in the house to help her. In utter frustration, Daneysha sat on the floor and cried.

Then she began to sing some old 70s' tunes and eventually a song from the Beatles about Mother Mary's coming to us when we find ourselves in trouble.

That was when it happened; one of those insights that only come when a person is at their wits' end.

The babe in her arms was named Jesu Alejandro. Jesus.

It was Palm Sunday, and Daneysha realized that the person Mary saw enter Jerusalem was no king. Riding on that donkey was the baby Mary had held in her arms, bathed in cold water, cried over in frustration and helplessness.

Daneysha knew that the Passion story would never be the same for her again.

King of glory, you were strong and mighty as you entered the ancient portals. Strengthen me. You were weak and vulnerable as your mother held you in her arms. Soften me. All is holy.

Today, find an image of strength in weakness.

///////////////////

to live unafraid

The LORD is my light and my salvation;
whom shall I fear?
The LORD is the stronghold of my life;
of whom shall I be afraid?

When evildoers assail me
to devour my flesh—
my adversaries and foes—
they shall stumble and fall.

Though an army encamp against me,
my heart shall not fear;
though war rise up against me,
yet I will be confident.

One thing I asked of the LORD,
that will I seek after:
to live in the house of the LORD
all the days of my life,
to behold the beauty of the LORD,
and to inquire in his temple.

For he will hide me in his shelter
in the day of trouble;
he will conceal me under the cover of his tent;
he will set me high on a rock.

Elizabeth was determined to help her children finish school. One day she learned that the grade school students were planning a field trip and her son needed $2.50 for lunch and the bus.

Elizabeth went through the things in her house, put some possible "extras" outside, and held a rummage sale to raise the money. When she had enough, she brought everything back into the house until the next time.

Elizabeth knew the field trip was one small step toward furthering her son's education. More important, she wanted him to feel like he belonged with the rest of his class.

Elizabeth knew the time would come when her children would need to worry about food and housing and school supplies, but for now she wanted them to live unafraid among their friends. Though faced with monumental challenges, she trusted that the Lord would ultimately take care of her family.

Elizabeth met each day with a warrior's strength and a mother's love, trusting she would receive all she needed for that one day.

Ever-provident God, enlarge my heart to receive your bountiful gifts. Humble my pride so that I may rely on you and your people. Stir my apathy to care about the many who live on the margins of society.

Today, look through your home and find two things you can do without. Share them with others.

///////////////

to forgive

Happy are those whose transgression is forgiven,
whose sin is covered.
Happy are those to whom the Lord imputes no iniquity,
and in whose spirit there is no deceit.

While I kept silence, my body wasted away
through my groaning all day long.
For day and night your hand was heavy upon me;
my strength was dried up as by the heat of summer.

Then I acknowledged my sin to you,
and I did not hide my iniquity;
I said, "I will confess my transgressions to the Lord,"
and you forgave the guilt of my sin.

Therefore let all who are faithful
offer prayer to you;
at a time of distress, the rush of mighty waters
shall not reach them.
You are a hiding place for me;
you preserve me from trouble;
you surround me with glad cries of deliverance.

PSALM 32:1–7

The first time at the prison was unforgettable. Chaplain Dan was brought into an empty room and left to wait for whoever chose to come. In preparation for the worship service, he had reflected prayerfully on the Scripture selection. He had chosen hymns he hoped would be familiar to the inmates.

Dan asked one inmate what he wanted to hear from the sermon, and the inmate calmly said, "Pastor, tell me something that will be meaningful when they close the bars on me and I'm all alone."

Day and night the prisoners feel the heavy hand of their guilt. Holding their wrongdoings to themselves, they can become tormented and angry in the long hours of solitude.

Allowing God to come into their personal darkness brings a light that reveals that goodness in great abundance exists within them too. It is the goodness of God.

This is a meaningful message all men and women need to hear.

Forgiving God, I have sinned. Look upon the offenses I have committed and forgive me. Look upon the offenses I have experienced and heal me. Fill me with your abundant power and grace.

Today, contact someone with whom you feel separated.

PSALM 51

to be washed clean

Have mercy on me, O God,
according to your steadfast love;
according to your abundant mercy
blot out my transgressions.
Wash me thoroughly from my iniquity,
and cleanse me from my sin.

For I know my transgressions,
and my sin is ever before me.
Against you, you alone, have I sinned,
and done what is evil in your sight,
so that you are justified in your sentence
and blameless when you pass judgment.
Indeed, I was born guilty,
a sinner when my mother conceived me.

You desire truth in the inward being;
therefore teach me wisdom in my secret heart.
Purge me with hyssop, and I shall be clean;
wash me, and I shall be whiter than snow.
Let me hear joy and gladness;
let the bones that you have crushed rejoice.

PSALM 51:1–8

Sophia held Abigail, bathed her, and fed her at the Central American Home for Malnourished Infants. Rescued from a dumpster as a newborn, Abigail was a fighter, surrounded by people fighting with her. As Sophia whispered to Abigail of her beauty, she sent out a prayer for her mother.

A woman must be devastatingly desperate to abandon a child that way. No one knows the sin and violence in which this tiny baby may have been conceived; no one knows the filth and darkness in which she was born.

But God knows. And in his merciful love, he has washed away the mother's transgressions.

God knows. And through the hands of Sophia, he has washed away the dirt and death into which she was born.

God knows. And when you and I experience ourselves as totally vulnerable, abandoned, and standing naked in our guilt, God washes us clean so that we are no longer crushed.

Compassionate God, hold me close and wash away all that is lifeless within me. Cleanse me from voices that subdue your words of gladness and joy. Heal me of past memories that rob me of present gifts. May your mercy, O Lord, rest upon me.

Today, hold a child.
Whisper a prayer for infant and mother.

/////////////////////

to walk in light

This I know, that God is for me.
In God, whose word I praise,
in the LORD, whose word I praise,
in God I trust; I am not afraid.
What can a mere mortal do to me?

My vows to you I must perform, O God;
I will render thank offerings to you.
For you have delivered my soul from death,
and my feet from falling,
so that I may walk before God
in the light of life.

PSALM 56:9–13

Maria was standing in the airport lobby with her mother and father. At 16, this was her first major trip alone. She was going away for an entire month. She was going to fly for the first time. She was representing her state at a gathering of Girl Scouts from around the nation.

Maria was dressed in her Girl Scout green; green slack suit, green beret, and green sash that displayed her many badges. Her sunglasses were an attempt to cover the tears forming in her eyes, though Maria's trembling voice exposed the fear she was so desperately trying to hide. "How will they know me when I arrive in Oklahoma?" she asked.

Her parents looked at their green-clad daughter, concealed the temptation to laugh, and answered, "I'm sure they will recognize you from the photo you sent."

"How will they know me" and what I believe?

"How will they know me" and that I trust in God?

"How will they know me" unless I walk in the light?

Radiant Lord, may I walk this day in your light. May I walk in such a way that I bring your light to those I meet along the way. May I be known by the brightness that my words and deeds bring into the world in which I live.

Today, sit in the darkness with only a candle as your light.

to be poured out

For God alone my soul waits in silence;
from him comes my salvation.
He alone is my rock and my salvation,
my fortress; I shall never be shaken.

How long will you assail a person,
will you batter your victim, all of you,
as you would a leaning wall, a tottering fence?
Their only plan is to bring down a person of prominence.
They take pleasure in falsehood;
they bless with their mouths,
but inwardly they curse.

For God alone my soul waits in silence,
for my hope is from him.
He alone is my rock and my salvation,
my fortress; I shall not be shaken.
On God rests my deliverance and my honor;
my mighty rock, my refuge is in God.

Trust in him at all times, O people;
pour out your heart before him;
God is a refuge for us.

PSALM 62:1–8

Brian was a member of a local peace-and-justice community. They had decided to purchase a house within a dangerous neighborhood. They also decided to gather for daily prayer and an evening meal and invite the nearby street people. They believed their presence would slowly transform the neighborhood.

One night as Brian was on his way to their gathering, he saw a woman scrubbing the sidewalk. Candles were lit and placed around the area she was cleaning. A spirit of reverence was present as she scrubbed.

The woman explained that a young man had been murdered at that spot on the previous evening. Police tape had been removed, another incident report of gang violence had been filed, and a crime-watch warning had gone out to the local area. All that remained now was the stain of blood on the sidewalk. This was the mark she was respectfully clearing away. The mark of a life lost.

There are times when violence seems to be winning.

But there are people who continue to pour themselves out so this doesn't happen.

> **God, our refuge, bless the peacemakers who seek to be an island of gentleness in the midst of violence. Bless them with vision and perseverance. Bless them with strength and courage. Bless us with the willingness to stand as one with them.**

Today, practice nonviolence.

to be carried

Let God rise up, let his enemies be scattered;
let those who hate him flee before him.
As smoke is driven away, so drive them away;
as wax melts before the fire,
let the wicked perish before God.
But let the righteous be joyful;
let them exult before God;
let them be jubilant with joy.

Sing to God, sing praises to his name;
lift up a song to him who rides upon the clouds—
his name is the LORD—
be exultant before him.

Father of orphans and protector of widows
is God in his holy habitation.
God gives the desolate a home to live in;
he leads out the prisoners to prosperity,
but the rebellious live in a parched land.

PSALM 68:1–6

Little Benjamin was mesmerized by the large crucifix in the convent hallway. It was placed far higher than he could reach, so he called to his dad for help.

His father, John, lifted him up, carried his young son closer to the crucifix, then watched Benjamin tenderly touch each nail wound. "An owie," he repeated four times as he touched Jesus' hands and feet.

When Benjamin reached out and touched the wound in Jesus' side, he did so with his entire hand. Then, without saying a word, Benjamin leaned forward and kissed the wound.

Had Benjamin not been carried by his father, he could not have touched the wounds.

Had Benjamin not been carried by his father, Jesus could not have received the healing kiss of a two-year-old boy.

Father of orphans and protector of widows, carry me in my weakness. Hold me as I touch the wounds of my own life and seek healing. I join with your Son, Jesus, that by his wounds we may heal a broken world.

Today, gaze upon a crucifix.
Reflectively touch each wound.

PSALM 73
///////////////////

to be near God

I am continually with you;
you hold my right hand.
You guide me with your counsel,
and afterward you will receive me with honor.
Whom have I in heaven but you?
And there is nothing on earth that I desire other than you.
My flesh and my heart may fail,
but God is the strength of my heart and my portion forever.

Indeed, those who are far from you will perish;
you put an end to those who are false to you.
But for me it is good to be near God;
I have made the Lord GOD my refuge.

PSALM 73:23–28

J oanne was an impressive woman—tall, stately in bearing, well educated, articulate, and a lifelong leader. Her friend Kathleen visited daily during the weeks she was hospitalized, bringing news of community events, small samples of her favorite foods, and interruptions of life into the quiet of her impending death.

On that final day, Kathleen bounced in and asked what she could do for her friend. Pray the Scriptures? Did she want some ice or, better yet, some ice cream? But on that final day, Joanne simply whispered, "Stay." Kathleen stayed. Throughout the night, she would lean close and whisper, "Joanne, this is your friend. I'm staying."

These were the final words she heard, their final promise of friendship. They had passed beyond the time when anything could be done. They had even passed beyond the need to do anything.

Together, the friends kept silent vigil on this last sacred moment of their journey.

"Stay with me" Jesus asked of his friends in the Garden of Gethsemane.

"Stay with us" requested the devastated apostles on the road to Emmaus.

"Stay" is our most profound invitation.

> **Faithful God, I have set so many requests before you, but the deepest longing of my heart is for your very self. Stay with me always. Hold my hand, be the rock of my heart, and receive me in glory. With anything less, I should always be in want.**

Today, go for a walk.
Let God take hold of your right hand.

PSALM 87
//////////////////

to belong

On the holy mount stands the city he founded;
the Lord loves the gates of Zion
more than all the dwellings of Jacob.
Glorious things are spoken of you,
O city of God.

Among those who know me I mention Rahab and Babylon;
Philistia too, and Tyre, with Ethiopia—
"This one was born there," they say.

And of Zion it shall be said,
"This one and that one were born in it";
for the Most High himself will establish it.
The Lord records, as he registers the peoples,
"This one was born there."

Psalm 87:1–6

Chris sat quietly at the side of his sister, Lijuan, who had just arrived from China with her adoptive parents. Vibrant and following the many unfamiliar sounds in her new environment, Lijuan clutched the red candy box that attracted her attention. She was totally present.

Though watching intently, Chris seemed to be far off in his thoughts. Finally, out came the words, "I'm thinking that in China, Lijuan just might have another brother or sister. I know she has a mom and dad and grandparents. That means I'm related to people I will never meet. Until, of course, we get to heaven."

On the holy mountain stands the city God has founded.

The Lord loves that city more than all the other dwellings, because in that city we will finally get to meet all our relatives.

We will find that we are all related.

God of all peoples, help us remember that we all belong to one great family. We are blessed with brothers and sisters who are different than us in language, homeland, and foods. We are blessed with brothers and sisters who are the same as us in their desire to love and be loved. What a wonderful, blessed family!

Today, learn to say hello in another language.

PSALM 102
///////////////////

to seek voice

For my days pass away like smoke,
and my bones burn like a furnace.
My heart is stricken and withered like grass;
I am too wasted to eat my bread.
Because of my loud groaning
my bones cling to my skin.
I am like an owl of the wilderness,
like a little owl of the waste places.
I lie awake;
I am like a lonely bird on the housetop.
All day long my enemies taunt me;
those who deride me use my name for a curse.
For I eat ashes like bread,
and mingle tears with my drink,
because of your indignation and anger;
for you have lifted me up and thrown me aside.
My days are like an evening shadow;
I wither away like grass.

PSALM 102:3–11

J ulia was always impressed by people who could converse with ease at social events. She felt trapped in her life situation. Her husband kept her walking a fine, careful line concerning what was acceptable and was quick to tell her what was not.

If she talked about God, her husband told her she was acting holier-than-thou.

If she talked about her family, she feared being accused of telling family secrets.

If she asked about other people, her husband called her nosy.

Like a lonely bird on the housetop, Julia stayed busy and tried not to think about it. In her imagination, she was intelligent and valued. In her imagination, she was the daughter of the God who created her. In her imagination, she was vibrant and alive.

In her life, she was withering like the grass.

Renewer of life, help me to be sensitive to those who suffer in silence. May I listen so that all people are freed to speak the wisdom of their own experience in their own voice.
May I listen with the ear of my heart.

Today, listen.

PSALM 123

////////////////////////

to lift up

To you I lift up my eyes,
O you who are enthroned in the heavens!
As the eyes of servants
look to the hand of their master,
as the eyes of a maid
to the hand of her mistress,
so our eyes look to the LORD our God,
until he has mercy upon us.

Have mercy upon us, O LORD, have mercy upon us,
for we have had more than enough of contempt.

Our soul has had more than its fill
of the scorn of those who are at ease,
of the contempt of the proud.

Aurora was preparing to defend her doctoral dissertation as she made breakfast for her family. She realized she was not being fully attentive to her children, and finally she stopped and said, "Kids, I need your prayers because I am getting ready for a big test."

Her daughter Jayda queried, "What is your test about, Mom?"

Aurora scrambled to translate what a degree in theology meant into the language of a preschooler and said, "It's about God."

"Why, Mommy, that's easy," offered Jayda. "God lives in the clouds in heaven, and if we just plant some beans in our garden, they will grow so high we can climb up and visit God."

Jayda's theology may be simple, but her God is real.

She could indeed lift up her eyes and know God is close at hand.

Most High Lord, come down and walk among us once again. We need to see you with the eyes of a child. We need to free you from our complicated notions of who you are. We need to fill our eyes and hearts and minds with the knowledge that you are intimately real.

Today, visit with a child and talk about God.

PSALM 127

//////////////////

to nurture

Unless the LORD *builds the house,*
those who build it labor in vain.
Unless the LORD *guards the city,*
the guard keeps watch in vain.
It is in vain that you rise up early
and go late to rest,
eating the bread of anxious toil;
for he gives sleep to his beloved.

Sons are indeed a heritage from the LORD,
the fruit of the womb a reward.
Like arrows in the hand of a warrior
are the sons of one's youth.
Happy is the man who has
his quiver full of them.
He shall not be put to shame
when he speaks with his enemies in the gate.

At first, Brianna defies the image of young people in foster care. She is an honor student, sings in the school choir, and works part time. Her favorite class is Latin. She dreams of studying environmental engineering.

But first glances can be deceiving. In the past year, both of Brianna's parents were murdered. The relative with whom she went to live died a few months after Brianna moved in.

Since her parents' death, Brianna has lived in five different placement homes as strangers try to figure out what to do with her. Brianna became a child of the courts, because she has anger issues and had begun to run around with some tough kids. Brianna is 15.

Unless the Lord builds the house, they labor in vain who build.

Unless a child has someone who cares, they live in disarray and turmoil.

Unless Brianna finds stability, she will not fulfill her dreams.

Keeper of promises, I thank you for the people who have nurtured me throughout my life. May all who guided my early steps and youthful dreams be blessed. May my gratitude overflow into loving action to those who are young and alone.

Today, research the number of children awaiting adoption or foster-care placement. Pray they will find a home.

PSALM 133

to be together

How very good and pleasant it is
when kindred live together in unity!
It is like the precious oil on the head,
running down upon the beard,
on the beard of Aaron,
running down over the collar of his robes.
It is like the dew of Hermon,
which falls on the mountains of Zion.
For there the LORD *ordained his blessing,*
life forevermore.

The phone rang loudly in the middle of the night. It woke Pat from a deep sleep, though not the ringing phone so much as the harsh, angry voice on the other end.

"Who do you think you are?" shouted the caller.

"Who in God's name do you think you are to speak out against the execution of that murderer?"

Without taking a moment to prepare his response, Pat simply answered, "I am a child of God and a brother to every other child of God. That includes my brother who was executed tonight. It includes the people he murdered many years ago. It includes you."

Hanging up the receiver, Pat turned back to sleep with the realization that he had just spoken a profound truth. To dwell together as one is not easy; it is not always good and pleasant.

However, it is who we are.

Hope of the world, we struggle to live as a global family. Guide us in peace and understanding. Remind us that we are your children and therefore connected to every other person as a brother or a sister.

Today, learn about another culture. Thank God for the diversity of the human family.

PSALM 139

////////////////////

to receive care

For it was you who formed my inward parts;
you knit me together in my mother's womb.
I praise you, for I am fearfully and wonderfully made.
Wonderful are your works;
that I know very well.
My frame was not hidden from you,
when I was being made in secret,
intricately woven in the depths of the earth.
Your eyes beheld my unformed substance.
In your book were written
all the days that were formed for me,
when none of them as yet existed.
How weighty to me are your thoughts, O God!
How vast is the sum of them!
I try to count them—they are more than the sand;
I come to the end—I am still with you.

PSALM 139:13–18

Sharon was building homes in Guatemala, and her group was eating breakfast when an elderly woman came to beg at the door. As she walked on, Sharon picked up her waffle and syrup packets and followed. Then they sat on the curb and ate in comfortable silence, broken by soft laughter when syrup would run down one of their hands or chin.

Though it was a busy morning, a man stopped long enough to say in English, "You are a beautiful woman." Sharon translated it for her barefoot, syrup-smeared friend with a smile and a gesture that said, "He said we are beautiful women. Isn't that wonderful? And it's true!"

The elderly woman's beauty will never make it to the front cover of a magazine. It will often come crusted with dirt and secondhand clothing. It will come from an inner strength that quietly proclaims, "I am precious to God. I am intimately known by God. I am beautiful in God's eyes."

Creator God, open my eyes to the beauty you have placed in each person I meet. You tenderly formed each one of us; you care for each person as precious and treasured. Help me to care as you care.

Today, take something of beauty, flowers, cookies, a pretty quilt, to a shelter for abused women.

CONCLUSION

AN INVITATION

The LORD is near to all who call on him,
to all who call on him in truth.

PSALM 145:18

THERE ARE MANY more psalms to be explored in this ancient book of the believing community, a myriad of verses awaiting your lingering gaze. There is at least one more very important reflection to be written—it is the one you are invited to write from the truth of your own life.

Delve into the psalms and allow yourself to be led to a verse or a word. Then illuminate and expand on it with your own story and prayer. Truly believe the Lord is near as you walk the daily journey that is your unique path in life.

Live in faith, hope, and love.

Speak your truth.

Walk with God.

God is always there.